Guests

Name and relationship to parents

_____

_____

Advice for parents

_____

_____

_____

Wishes for baby

_____

_____

_____

_____

Guests

Name and relationship to parents

_____

_____

Advice for parents

_____

_____

_____

_____

Wishes for baby

_____

_____

_____

_____

Guests

Name and relationship to parents

_____

_____

Advice for parents

_____

_____

_____

_____

Wishes for baby

_____

_____

_____

_____

Guests

Name and relationship to parents

_____

_____

Advice for parents

_____

_____

_____

_____

Wishes for baby

_____

_____

_____

_____

Guests

Name and relationship to parents

_____

_____

Advice for parents

_____

_____

_____

_____

Wishes for baby

_____

_____

_____

_____

Guests

Name and relationship to parents

_____

_____

Advice for parents

_____

_____

_____

_____

Wishes for baby

_____

_____

_____

_____

Guests

Name and relationship to parents

_____

_____

Advice for parents

_____

_____

_____

_____

Wishes for baby

_____

_____

_____

_____

Guests

Name and relationship to parents

_____

_____

Advice for parents

_____

_____

_____

_____

Wishes for baby

_____

_____

_____

_____

Guests

Name and relationship to parents

_____

_____

Advice for parents

_____

_____

_____

_____

Wishes for baby

_____

_____

_____

_____

Guests

Name and relationship to parents

_____

_____

Advice for parents

_____

_____

_____

_____

Wishes for baby

_____

_____

_____

_____

Guests

Name and relationship to parents

_____

_____

Advice for parents

_____

_____

_____

_____

Wishes for baby

_____

_____

_____

_____

Guests

Name and relationship to parents

_____

_____

Advice for parents

_____

_____

_____

_____

Wishes for baby

_____

_____

_____

_____

Guests

Name and relationship to parents

_____

_____

Advice for parents

_____

_____

_____

_____

Wishes for baby

_____

_____

_____

_____

Guests

Name and relationship to parents

_____

_____

Advice for parents

_____

_____

_____

Wishes for baby

_____

_____

_____

Guests

Name and relationship to parents

_____

_____

Advice for parents

_____

_____

_____

_____

Wishes for baby

_____

_____

_____

_____

Guests

Name and relationship to parents

_____

_____

Advice for parents

_____

_____

_____

_____

Wishes for baby

_____

_____

_____

_____

Guests

Name and relationship to parents

_____

_____

Advice for parents

_____

_____

_____

_____

Wishes for baby

_____

_____

_____

_____

Guests

Name and relationship to parents

_____

_____

Advice for parents

_____

_____

_____

_____

Wishes for baby

_____

_____

_____

_____

Guests

Name and relationship to parents

_____

_____

Advice for parents

_____

_____

_____

_____

Wishes for baby

_____

_____

_____

_____

Guests

Name and relationship to parents

_____

_____

Advice for parents

_____

_____

_____

_____

Wishes for baby

_____

_____

_____

_____

Guests

Name and relationship to parents

_____

_____

Advice for parents

_____

_____

_____

_____

Wishes for baby

_____

_____

_____

_____

Guests

Name and relationship to parents

_____

_____

Advice for parents

_____

_____

_____

Wishes for baby

_____

_____

_____

_____

Guests

Name and relationship to parents

_____

_____

Advice for parents

_____

_____

_____

_____

Wishes for baby

_____

_____

_____

_____

Guests

Name and relationship to parents

_____

_____

Advice for parents

_____

_____

_____

_____

Wishes for baby

_____

_____

_____

_____

Guests

Name and relationship to parents

_____

_____

Advice for parents

_____

_____

_____

_____

Wishes for baby

_____

_____

_____

_____

Guests

Name and relationship to parents

_____

_____

Advice for parents

_____

_____

_____

Wishes for baby

_____

_____

_____

Guests

Name and relationship to parents

_____

_____

Advice for parents

_____

_____

_____

_____

Wishes for baby

_____

_____

_____

_____

Guests

Name and relationship to parents

_____

_____

Advice for parents

_____

_____

_____

_____

Wishes for baby

_____

_____

_____

_____

Guests

Name and relationship to parents

_____

_____

Advice for parents

_____

_____

_____

_____

Wishes for baby

_____

_____

_____

_____

Guests

Name and relationship to parents

_____

_____

Advice for parents

_____

_____

_____

_____

Wishes for baby

_____

_____

_____

_____

Guests

Name and relationship to parents

_____

_____

Advice for parents

_____

_____

_____

_____

Wishes for baby

_____

_____

_____

_____

Guests

Name and relationship to parents

_____

_____

Advice for parents

_____

_____

_____

_____

Wishes for baby

_____

_____

_____

_____

Guests

Name and relationship to parents

_____

_____

Advice for parents

_____

_____

_____

_____

Wishes for baby

_____

_____

_____

_____

Guests

Name and relationship to parents

_____

_____

Advice for parents

_____

_____

_____

_____

Wishes for baby

_____

_____

_____

_____

Guests

Name and relationship to parents

_____

_____

Advice for parents

_____

_____

_____

_____

Wishes for baby

_____

_____

_____

_____

Guests

Name and relationship to parents

_____

_____

Advice for parents

_____

_____

_____

_____

Wishes for baby

_____

_____

_____

_____

Guests

Name and relationship to parents

_____

_____

Advice for parents

_____

_____

_____

_____

Wishes for baby

_____

_____

_____

_____

Guests

Name and relationship to parents

_____

_____

Advice for parents

_____

_____

_____

_____

Wishes for baby

_____

_____

_____

_____

Guests

Name and relationship to parents

_____

_____

Advice for parents

_____

_____

_____

_____

Wishes for baby

_____

_____

_____

_____

Guests

Name and relationship to parents

_____

_____

Advice for parents

_____

_____

_____

Wishes for baby

_____

_____

_____

Guests

Name and relationship to parents

_____

_____

Advice for parents

_____

_____

_____

Wishes for baby

_____

_____

_____

Guests

Name and relationship to parents

_____

_____

Advice for parents

_____

_____

_____

_____

Wishes for baby

_____

_____

_____

_____

Guests

Name and relationship to parents

_____

_____

Advice for parents

_____

_____

_____

_____

Wishes for baby

_____

_____

_____

_____

Guests

Name and relationship to parents

_____

_____

Advice for parents

_____

_____

_____

Wishes for baby

_____

_____

_____

Guests

Name and relationship to parents

_____

_____

Advice for parents

_____

_____

_____

_____

Wishes for baby

_____

_____

_____

_____

Guests

Name and relationship to parents

_____

_____

Advice for parents

_____

_____

_____

_____

Wishes for baby

_____

_____

_____

_____

Guests

Name and relationship to parents

_____

_____

Advice for parents

_____

_____

_____

_____

Wishes for baby

_____

_____

_____

_____

Guests

Name and relationship to parents

_____

_____

Advice for parents

_____

_____

_____

Wishes for baby

_____

_____

_____

Guests

Name and relationship to parents

_____

_____

Advice for parents

_____

_____

_____

_____

Wishes for baby

_____

_____

_____

_____

Guests

Name and relationship to parents

_____

_____

Advice for parents

_____

_____

_____

Wishes for baby

_____

_____

_____

_____

Guests

Name and relationship to parents

_____

_____

Advice for parents

_____

_____

_____

_____

Wishes for baby

_____

_____

_____

_____

Guests

Name and relationship to parents

_____

_____

Advice for parents

_____

_____

_____

_____

Wishes for baby

_____

_____

_____

_____

Guests

Name and relationship to parents

_____

_____

Advice for parents

_____

_____

_____

_____

Wishes for baby

_____

_____

_____

_____

Guests

Name and relationship to parents

_____

_____

Advice for parents

_____

_____

_____

_____

Wishes for baby

_____

_____

_____

_____

Guests

Name and relationship to parents

_____

_____

Advice for parents

_____

_____

_____

_____

Wishes for baby

_____

_____

_____

_____

Guests

Name and relationship to parents

_____

_____

Advice for parents

_____

_____

_____

Wishes for baby

_____

_____

_____

Guests

Name and relationship to parents

_____

_____

Advice for parents

_____

_____

_____

_____

Wishes for baby

_____

_____

_____

_____

Guests

Name and relationship to parents

_____

_____

Advice for parents

_____

_____

_____

Wishes for baby

_____

_____

_____

Guests

Name and relationship to parents

_____

_____

Advice for parents

_____

_____

_____

Wishes for baby

_____

_____

_____

Guests

Name and relationship to parents

_____

_____

Advice for parents

_____

_____

_____

Wishes for baby

_____

_____

_____

Guests

Name and relationship to parents

_____

_____

Advice for parents

_____

_____

_____

_____

Wishes for baby

_____

_____

_____

_____

Guests

Name and relationship to parents

_____

_____

Advice for parents

_____

_____

_____

_____

Wishes for baby

_____

_____

_____

_____

Guests

Name and relationship to parents

_____

_____

Advice for parents

_____

_____

_____

_____

Wishes for baby

_____

_____

_____

_____

Guests

Name and relationship to parents

_____

_____

Advice for parents

_____

_____

_____

_____

Wishes for baby

_____

_____

_____

_____

Guests

Name and relationship to parents

_____

_____

Advice for parents

_____

_____

_____

_____

Wishes for baby

_____

_____

_____

_____

Guests

Name and relationship to parents

_____

_____

Advice for parents

_____

_____

_____

_____

Wishes for baby

_____

_____

_____

_____

Guests

Name and relationship to parents

_____

_____

Advice for parents

_____

_____

_____

_____

Wishes for baby

_____

_____

_____

_____

Guests

Name and relationship to parents

_____

_____

Advice for parents

_____

_____

_____

_____

Wishes for baby

_____

_____

_____

_____

Guests

Name and relationship to parents

_____

_____

Advice for parents

_____

_____

_____

_____

Wishes for baby

_____

_____

_____

_____

Guests

Name and relationship to parents

_____

_____

Advice for parents

_____

_____

_____

_____

Wishes for baby

_____

_____

_____

_____

Guests

Name and relationship to parents

_____

_____

Advice for parents

_____

_____

_____

_____

Wishes for baby

_____

_____

_____

_____

Guests

Name and relationship to parents

_____

_____

Advice for parents

_____

_____

_____

_____

Wishes for baby

_____

_____

_____

_____

Guests

Name and relationship to parents

_____

_____

Advice for parents

_____

_____

_____

_____

Wishes for baby

_____

_____

_____

_____

Guests

Name and relationship to parents

_____

_____

Advice for parents

_____

_____

_____

Wishes for baby

_____

_____

_____

Guests

Name and relationship to parents

_____

_____

Advice for parents

_____

_____

_____

_____

Wishes for baby

_____

_____

_____

_____

Guests

Name and relationship to parents

_____

_____

Advice for parents

_____

_____

_____

Wishes for baby

_____

_____

_____

Guests

Name and relationship to parents

_____

_____

Advice for parents

_____

_____

_____

Wishes for baby

_____

_____

_____

Guests

Name and relationship to parents

_____

_____

Advice for parents

_____

_____

_____

_____

Wishes for baby

_____

_____

_____

_____

Guests

Name and relationship to parents

_____

_____

Advice for parents

_____

_____

_____

_____

Wishes for baby

_____

_____

_____

_____

Guests

Name and relationship to parents

_____

_____

Advice for parents

_____

_____

_____

_____

Wishes for baby

_____

_____

_____

_____

Guests

Name and relationship to parents

_____

_____

Advice for parents

_____

_____

_____

_____

Wishes for baby

_____

_____

_____

_____

Guests

Name and relationship to parents

_____

_____

Advice for parents

_____

_____

_____

_____

Wishes for baby

_____

_____

_____

_____

Guests

Name and relationship to parents

_____

_____

Advice for parents

_____

_____

_____

_____

Wishes for baby

_____

_____

_____

_____

Guests

Name and relationship to parents

_____

_____

Advice for parents

_____

_____

_____

_____

Wishes for baby

_____

_____

_____

_____

Guests

Name and relationship to parents

_____

_____

Advice for parents

_____

_____

_____

Wishes for baby

_____

_____

_____

_____

Guests

Name and relationship to parents

_____

_____

Advice for parents

_____

_____

_____

Wishes for baby

_____

_____

_____

Guests

Name and relationship to parents

_____

_____

Advice for parents

_____

_____

_____

_____

Wishes for baby

_____

_____

_____

_____

Guests

Name and relationship to parents

_____

_____

Advice for parents

_____

_____

_____

Wishes for baby

_____

_____

_____

Guests

Name and relationship to parents

_____

_____

Advice for parents

_____

_____

_____

Wishes for baby

_____

_____

_____

_____

Guests

Name and relationship to parents

_____

_____

Advice for parents

_____

_____

_____

_____

Wishes for baby

_____

_____

_____

_____

Gift log

Gift	Given by

Gift log

Gift	Given by
_____	_____
_____	_____
_____	_____
_____	_____
_____	_____
_____	_____
_____	_____
_____	_____
_____	_____
_____	_____

Gift   Given by

_____   _____

_____   _____

_____   _____

_____   _____

_____   _____

_____   _____

_____   _____

_____   _____

_____   _____

_____   _____

_____   _____

_____   _____

Gift log

Gift	Given by

Gift log

Gift   Given by

_____   _____

_____   _____

_____   _____

_____   _____

_____   _____

_____   _____

_____   _____

_____   _____

_____   _____

_____   _____

_____   _____

Gift log

Gift	Given by
_____	_____
_____	_____
_____	_____
_____	_____
_____	_____
_____	_____
_____	_____
_____	_____
_____	_____
_____	_____

Gift

Given by

_____

_____

_____

_____

_____

_____

_____

_____

_____

_____

_____

_____

_____

_____

_____

_____

_____

_____

_____

_____

_____

_____

Gift log

Gift	Given by
_____	_____
_____	_____
_____	_____
_____	_____
_____	_____
_____	_____
_____	_____
_____	_____
_____	_____
_____	_____
_____	_____

Gift log

Gift	Given by

Gift log

Gift	Given by
_____	_____
_____	_____
_____	_____
_____	_____
_____	_____
_____	_____
_____	_____
_____	_____
_____	_____
_____	_____
_____	_____
_____	_____

Special memories

Special memories

Special memories

Special memories

Special memories

Special memories

Special memories

Special memories

Special memories

Special memories

Made in the USA
Columbia, SC
15 April 2025

56648476R00069